LOW CARB FOOD LIST

Best Foods to Eat on a Low Carb Diet Along with a Meal Plan, for Healthy Living and Weight Loss

Nancy Peterson

Copyright@2019

TABLE OF CONTENTS

Introduction 3

CHAPTER 1 5

What Is a Low-Carb Diet? 5

Health Benefits of Low-Carb Diets.............16

Common Misinformation about Low-Carb
Diets 18

CHAPTER 2...23

Getting Started 23

How Much Carbohydrate is Enough?.........24

Different Food Types and The Carbs
Contained in Them 25

What to Eat when Eating Out 35

Your Shopping List for Low Carb Diet 36

CHAPTER 3...39

List of Low Carb Foods that are Healthy and
Taste Incredible..39

CHAPTER 4...69

7 Days Low-Carb Menu Plan.......................69

CHAPTER 5...74

Conclusion 74

Introduction

The popularity of Low-Carb Diet plans has increased in recent times due to how easy it is to follow. It also offers quick and painless solutions to health-related issues such as the prevention of diabetes, sluggishness, and fatigue. Keeping up with a Low-Carb Diet plan could even help with the regulation of your blood sugar, stop your cravings for sugar, and even help restore the hormones which give both appetites and the satisfactory feeling after each meal. Consequently, this will help you lose weight, reduce the chances of you being diabetic, increase your energy, and improve your general mood.

There are usually little to no limitations in terms of number of calories, fat, sodium, or cholesterol you should consume in most Low-Carb diets, which makes them more appealing as you don't have to worry about taking in too much or too less calories in a day. A Low-Carb Diet reduces the amount of carbohydrates you should take daily. This limitation usually ranges between 50 to 100 grams, and depends greatly on your size, activity level, and other factors.

Contrary to popular belief that Low-Carb Diet plans require that one gives up the food they love, you will find out as you read here that this is not true. Here you will find a detailed explanation of what Low-Carb Diets are, how they work, and meal plans to guide you through your Low-Carb Diet journey.

This book will also help you make simple and quick, yet fully delicious low-carb meals.

These Low-Carb Diets are most famous amongst people who seek to lose weight. Before starting a Low-Carb Diet plan, most people have said that the reason why they considered switching to it is because they suffered from decreased energy levels. This decrease is usually due to the increase in cravings for carb-heavy foods.

CHAPTER 1

What Is a Low-Carb Diet?

A low-Carbohydrate or Low-Carb Diet refers simply to diet plans in which the carbohydrate portions are reduced. Carbohydrate is a nutrient present in different types of food. These foods could be healthy or unhealthy amongst which includes dairy products, broccoli, soda, chocolate, potato, etc. It comes in many forms, the commonest of which includes starch, sugar and fiber.

One of the primary things one must consider when picking a Low-Carb Diet plan is finding a plan whose level suits you. The required amount of carbs a person should eat depends on the person as it varies between individuals. While most people should maintain a 20 percent or less caloric intake, about 2,000 calories are allowed for an average Low-Carb Diet; this is usually about 100 grams of carbohydrates daily.

How Does a Low-Carb Diet Work?

Basically, weight-loss diets reduce your overall intake of calories to a level which is actually required for your body. Similarly, Low-Carb Diets use the same method to bring about weight loss. Difference is, instead of telling you how much calories you should take; it normalizes your hormones and neurotransmitters which determine hunger, cravings, satiety and energy levels. This causes you to want only the required number of calories therefore losing excess weight.

To know how these carbs work, let's first take a look at how carbohydrate is usually broken-down during digestion. Like petrol to a car, Carbohydrates serve as energy to the body. The body breaks down carbohydrate intakes into simple sugar which are absorbed into the blood stream as glucose. This glucose is the blood sugar. Insulin then transports said glucose to the cells of one's body where it serves as energy. The excess glucose is converted to fat which is later used as a source of energy in situations where there's limited supply of carbohydrates. Now, all that Low-Carb Diet does is to limit the body's energy usage, thereby forcing the glucose-converted fat to be burned.

Now, when the excess glucose is being converted to fat, the calories contained in the fat can no longer serve as energy for the body. This causes your body to feel hungry even though you just ate, and the more you eat the more the glucose is converted to fat which only makes you hungry. The scientific explanation is: given to dieting on high-carbs food, your body produces insulin at an increased rate therefore increasing your biochemical drive to eat more whilst burning little energy.

When this happens, two other hormones in your body, Leptin and Ghrelin (which helps to regularize your appetite and to inform your brain when you're hungry or satisfied), won't function properly due to your overweight.

The Leptin is a hormone secreted in the fat cell with the primary objective of signalling your brain once the body has consumed enough fuel. Since it is situated in the fat cell, the fatter your body is, the more Leptin your body produces.

One would think that the more Leptin your body produces, the less hungry you should be; but this is not so. Turns out the Leptin is intercepted by the Insulin and is prevented from delivering its message to the brain. This causes you to eat continuously, which produces insulin, which creates more fat.

Ghrelin on the other hand is produced in the stomach with the main aim of alerting your brain when your stomach is hungry. The levels of Ghrelin increase when your body hasn't had any intake of food or, calories are supplied to your body in limited amounts. Most times, the Ghrelin works simultaneously with the Leptin; when you're hungry the Ghrelin increases and the Leptin decreases and vice versa.

Common remedies to maintain this balance include: not skipping meals, eating enough calories, avoiding fructose, consuming more portions of healthy fats.

Why Choose a Low-Carb Diet for Weight Loss?

Low-Carb Diets work. All of the above stated remedies are synonymous to starting a Low-Carb Diet. This is a major reason why low-carb diets are highly sort after. A calorie-restriction approach also works but it comes with issues which are absent in a Low-Carb Diet. Among these issues include being hungry due to reduced intake of calories. This causes you to succumb to eating;

consequently, leading to gaining back the weight you strived to lose.

How to Lose Weight on a Low-Carb Diet

In order to ensure success whilst following a Low-Carb Diet meal plan, it is recommended that you fully understand what carbohydrates are, the different types of carbohydrates and the rates at which they should be taken. Some carbohydrates are complex whereas others are simple. These can be easily explained using the terms 'Good Carbs' and 'Bad Carbs'.

Distinguishing between Good Carbs and Bad Carbs

Primarily, what makes good carbs differ from bad carbs is **Fiber**. Carbohydrates with less fiber are broken down quickly during digestion, and this quick breakdown brings about the sudden increase of blood sugar level as a result of large amounts of glucose being deposited at once in the bloodstream.

The good carbs, otherwise known as complex carbs, are absorbed into the system slowly since they are high in fiber. Sugar levels don't spike up on intake of high carbs, thus leading to the overproduction of insulin and Leptin resistance. The fiber in good carbs also helps your body stay content for longer periods of time with fewer calories.

Good or Complex Carbs can be found in:

- Whole grains (brown rice, oats, millet, bulgur)

- Beans and other legumes (black beans, pinto beans, peanuts)
- Fruits with no starch (berries, melons, apples, grapes, peaches, nectarines)
- Non-Starchy vegetables (leafy greens, broccoli, cauliflower, zucchini, cucumbers)

Bad or Simple carbs on the other hand, are plant foods which have had their valuable nutrients and fibrous contents stripped away through refinement; although some bad carbs lack fiber and nutrients naturally. Simple carbs also provide energy for the body, but that energy is short-lived and usually wears off if not used immediately for an energy-demanding task. Some of which include:

- Added sugar
- White rice
- White flour
- White potatoes
- White bread

Your choices of food would depend on some things like how often you exercise, your health status and how much weight you need to lose.

Based on this, tailor this meal plan according to the category you fall into.

Food you should Eat

Meat, eggs, fish, fruit, vegetables, nuts, high-fat dairy, seeds, healthy oils fats, and probably some tubers and non-gluten grains.

What you Should not Eat

HFCS, Sugar, wheat, trans fats, seed oils, low-fat products, "diet" and foods that are highly processed.

Health Benefits of Low-Carb Diets

Reducing your carbs intake would give tremendous health benefits. Not only will it reduce your hunger levels, it would also help you shed weight without the worries of counting calories.

Over 23 studies have proven that low carb diets produce more than 2 to 3 times weight loss results than low fat diets. You can tell that your blood sugar level is high when you experience symptoms such as: frequent hunger, thirst, frequent illness, fatigue, and frequent yeast infections.

It can also help in the reduction of blood-sugar, therefore lowering the chances of developing cancer, dementia, heart diseases, and diabetes. It ensures that your blood sugar level is stable, thus increasing energy and reducing cravings. Low-Carb diets lower insulin levels and resistance significantly, thus preventing cardiovascular diseases, high blood pressure, and stroke.

The blood levels of Triglycerides are lowered with a simultaneous increase in HDL (good) cholesterol, all thanks to Low-Carbs.

Also, it doesn't have to be stressful eating low carb meals. Simply work with whole foods that have low carb contents to help you lose unneeded fats and remain healthy.

Common Misinformation about Low-Carb Diets

Low-Carb Diets are often given a bad name due to some rumoured misgivings amongst which include:

- Low Carbs cause an increase in the risk of having heart diseases:

It's a common notion that low-carbs
may cause heart diseases given to how it
increases HDL cholesterol. They fear
that this cholesterol is bad for the
health; the heart in particular. This is
untrue given that Low-Carb Diets
reduces the amount of carbohydrates in
the body. This unavailability of
carbohydrates forces the fat to be
burned by the body in its quest for an
energy source.

- The side-effects of a Low-Carb
  Diet are Ketosis and Ketones:

Low-Carb Diets burn ketones alongside
with fat in a process called ketosis. The
ketones are produced during the
metabolism of fat and are used by bodily
cells, especially the brain cells. The
restriction of carbohydrates by Low-

Carb Diets does not raise ketones to levels that are harmful, although, ketones are higher in those who eat Low-Carb diets.

- You have to take both carbs and calories into account:

Low-Carb Diets create an organic reduction of calories. This helps you to lose weight without having to worry about how much calories are contained in the Low-Carb Diet meals.

- Carbohydrates is an essential nutrient:

People are often scared of being carb-deficit when they cut down their carb-intake. This is usually because they see carbohydrate as an essential nutrient. Nutrients such as protein and fatty acids are essential in that the body cannot produce them. The body can produce as much carbohydrates as it needs for energy, which makes it to not be an essential nutrient.

- You don't get all the nutrients you need from Low-Carb Diets:

This is untrue. A Low-Carb Diet based on whole foods most likely provides more vitamins, minerals, and fiber than standard diet plans. These whole foods include healthy fats, meats and vegetables.

- Osteoporosis and bone loss happen as a result of following a Low-Carb Diet:

Low-Carb Diets are usually high in fats (with protein served only in sufficient amounts). Although diets that are high in protein usually cause bone loss, diets with proteins served in sufficient amounts such as this one help maintain bone health; therefore, preventing osteoporosis.

- Kidney damage may occur

This is simply a belief which is built on the assumption that Low-Carb Diets are high in proteins. It is true that eating too much protein is bad for the kidney. However, Low-Carb Diets offer only a moderate amount of proteins which is safe.

CHAPTER 2

Getting Started

If you've read this far and are still interested in beginning a Low-Carb Diet meal plan; you've made the right choice. It could be quite menacing at first when you try to start a Low-Carb Diet, but if you follow this guide you should have no problems at all.

Low-Carb Diets can be healthy or unhealthy. This depends entirely on how you go about it. Before starting a low-carb diet, you need to ensure that you know everything about low-carbs. This will enable you create a plan (or follow a plan) which is tailored to suit your body.

How Much Carbohydrate is Enough?

There is really no defined rule that helps you know how many grams of carbohydrates you should eat. No two people are the same. Therefore, the amount of carbohydrates required by a person's body depends on many factors including: body composition, age, gender, activity level, and health conditions.

The gram per day for someone who already produces a lot of insulin is usually 40 grams or less. On the other hand, the grams-per-day for an active person can be as high as 100 grams.

For those who seek to lose weight, we recommend 50 to 100 grams per day. Foods such as vegetables with no starch, and certain fruits are still allowed when losing weight is the goal.

Figuring out what amount of carbs to take in daily is usually a 'see-what-works-for-me' type situation. We advise that you start out slow with about 50 grams per day, and work your way up. You need to track your body's adjustment to the carb intake. Take notes of how your weight changes, how your cravings increase or decrease, and how much food it takes to feel satisfied.

Different Food Types and The Carbs Contained in Them

When it comes to good carbs, it's best to pick carbohydrate-contained foods which offer you the most nutritional value. This includes whole grains, vegetables, and food made from whole grains. You should avoid bad carbs such as artificial sweeteners, refined sugar and white rice, at all costs.

It is important to know that artificial sweeteners aren't the same thing as caloric sweeteners. Caloric sweeteners include: honey, fruit, fruit juice, and maple syrup. Although they taste sweet, they contain no calories or carbs. This means they don't raise blood sugar or insulin levels; therefore, they are recommended for someone who is trying to lose weight.

There's a class of carbohydrates known as sugar alcohol (ironically, they are neither sugar nor alcohols). They are used as substitutes for sugar because they offer a bulk amount of low-calories sweetness. They don't get completely absorbed by the body during digestion. Consequently, the spikes in insulin and blood sugar levels after taking them are small. Sugar alcohols include maltitol, xylitol, erythritol, lactitol, and sorbitol.

You must have heard before now that alcoholic beverage such as red wine is good for your heart. Plants with high-carbs are usually used in the making of alcoholic beverages. The amount of sugar contained in alcoholic beverages differs. Dry wine contains very little sugar while sweet dessert wine contains a lot. Distilled spirits like vodka are always left with no carbs after fermentation. Liqueurs are the highest in terms of carbohydrate content; this is because they have added sugar.

In the body, alcohol is treated differently from carbohydrates; the calories that come with alcohol get burned first. If still you desire to take alcohol, it's best to stick to those that offer as little carbohydrates as possible; this includes dry wine or whiskey with non-caloric mixers.

It may seem like the rule book for Low-Carb Dieting is very thick, but I assure you it isn't. It's a simple 'what to eat' situation. First, focus on eating meat, eggs, fish, non-root vegetables, and natural fats.

Foods to Eat

You need to work your diet to include these unprocessed low carb foods.

- **Meat:** chicken, lamb, Beef, pork, and others; grass-fed is preferred.

- **Fish:** trout, Salmon, haddock and several others; The best is the wild-caught fish.

- **Eggs:** Either pastured eggs or Omega-3-enriched eggs are best.

- **Vegetables:** broccoli, Spinach, carrots, cauliflower and many others.

- **Fruits:** strawberries Apples, oranges, blueberries, pears.

- **Nuts and seeds:** Almonds, sunflower seeds, walnuts etc.

- **High-fat dairy:** heavy cream, butter, Cheese, yogurt.

- **Fats and oils:** butter, Coconut oil, lard, fish oil and olive oil.

If your goal is to shed excess weight, then watch how you consume nuts and cheese as its easy to consume more than needed. Limit your intake to one piece of fruit daily.

Foods that you May Include

If you are healthy, you exercise and your sole aim is not to lose weight, you can consume a little more carb.

- **Tubers:** sweet potatoes, Potatoes and some others.

- **Unrefined grains:** Oats, Brown rice, quinoa and many others.

- **Legumes:** black beans, Lentils, pinto beans, etc.

Also, you can consume the following in moderation if you like:

- **Dark chocolate:** It is important to go for organic brands that have minimum of 70% cocoa.

- **Wine:** Best are dry wines that have no extra sugar or carbs.

While Dark chocolate has high content of antioxidants and would be beneficial to the health if eater in appropriate quantity, however, excess consumption of it and alcohol can slow down your progress.

- Water

- Tea

- Coffee

- Carbonated beverages free of sugar like sparkling water.

Foods You Should Avoid

Below are six groups of food and nutrients you should avoid, written in their order of importance:

- **Sugar:** fruit juices, soft drinks, agave, ice cream candy, and several other products that have added sugar.

- **Refined grains:** Rice, rye, wheat, barley, Cereal, bread and pasta.

- **Trans fats:** partially hydrogenated or hydrogenated oils.

- **Diet and low-fat products:** Although several dairy products have low fat contents, however, they have extra sugar added.

- **Highly processed foods:** any food that looks like it is from a factory, it is best to avoid.

- **Starchy vegetables:** while on a low carb diet, its best to reduce your intake of starchy vegetables

While on the low carb diet, it is important you check every single ingredients' lists including those on foods with the "healthy food" label.

Healthy, Low-Carb Snacks

It is not advisable to consume more than three meals daily, however, you may get hungry occasionally in between meals. Below are lists of easy-to-prepare, healthy, low carb snacks that would make you filled:

- A piece of fruit

- One or two hard-boiled eggs

- Full-fat yogurt

- Leftovers from the previous night

- Baby carrots

- Some cheese and meat

- A grasp of nuts

What to Eat when Eating Out

If you have to eat out in restaurants, it is quite easy to order for low carb friendly meals.

- Let your main dish contain meat or fish.
- Take plain water instead of fruit juice or sugary soda.
- Request for more vegetables as against potatoes, bread or rice.

Your Shopping List for Low Carb Diet

An important rule is to limit your shopping to stores that has more of whole foods. Choosing whole foods will help you a thousand times more than the normal western diet.

Other choices include organic and grass-fed foods which are also healthy but are more expensive than the whole foods.

If you are on a budget, try to go for the option that has the least processed ingredients.

- Meat (bacon, beef, pork, lamb, chicken)

- Fish (fatty fish is preferred like salmon)

- Eggs (better to go with pastured eggs or choose omega-3 enriched eggs)

- Coconut oil

- Butter

- Lard

- Cheese

- Olive oil

- Heavy cream

- Yogurt (full-fat, unsweetened)

- Sour cream

- Blueberries (fresh or frozen)

- Olives

- Nuts

- Frozen vegetables (carrots, broccoli, and different combinations)
- Fresh vegetables (greens, onions, peppers etc.)
- Condiments (pepper, sea salt, mustard, garlic etc.)

Remove every unhealthy treat in your pantry that would limit you in reaching your goals. These include: sodas, ice cream, candy, chips, breads, juices and baking ingredients (sugar and refined flour)

CHAPTER 3

List of Low Carb Foods that are Healthy and Taste Incredible

Below you have 44 low carb meals that are not only healthy but are also nutritious and so delicious.

Net Carbs vs Total Carbs

At the each of each meal group, you would see the carb content for a serving size as well as the number of carbs available in a 100-gram portion.

However, it is important to note that several foods listed here have high fiber count and may reduce the digestible net carb content even more.

Eggs and every type of meat have nearly zero carb content with an exception to organ meats like liver that has about 5% carbs

Eggs

These are the most healthy and nutritious food found on the planet earth. They contain several nutrients some of which are important for your brain performance. They also contain compounds that help with better eye sights.

Carb count: Almost zero

Beef

Beef fills one up fast and has needed nutrients like vitamin B12 and iron. We have several types of meat like ground beef, ribeye steak, hamburger etc.

Carb content: zero.

Lamb

Similar to beef, this has several nutrients beneficial to the body which includes vitamin B12 and iron. Lamb could be grass-fed and so have high content of needed fatty acid.

Carb content: zero.

Chicken

Chicken is one of the most popular meats in the world. It is an excellent source of protein and also have several beneficial nutrients. While on the low carb diet, it may be better to go for sides with fats like the thighs and wings.

Carb content: zero.

Pork

This includes Bacon and is another delicious type of meat. Although bacon has been processed and cannot be counted as healthy meat, however, you can consume a moderate amount of it while on a low carb diet.

Source for the bacon locally to avoid artificial ingredients and ensure the bacon doesn't get burnt while cooking.

Carb content: zero (read labels to avoid bacon that has sugar)

Jerky

This is a type of meat cut into strips and dried. If it doesn't have any artificial ingredients or sugar then it is a good snack for low carb. It is important to state here that most of the jerky sold in stores have been highly processed and I would advise you make your jerky by yourself.

Carb content: close to zero if it is just meat and seasoning.

Other low carb meats include: Veal, Turkey, Bison and Venison.

SEAFOODS

Fish along with other seafoods are healthy and nutritious. They have high content of omega-3 fatty acids, iodine and vitamin B12, all of which is never enough in most cases.

Similar to meat, almost all fishy and seafood type has little or no carbs.

Salmon

This is one of the most popular type of fish for people who are health conscious. This is because of its high count of omega-3 fatty acids. Salmon is also high in iodine, Vitamin B12 along with a good amount of vitamin D3.

Carb content: zero.

Trout

Trout is another type of fish that has lots of fats and omega-3 fatty acids and several other important nutrients.

Carb content: zero.

Sardines

Sardines are oily fish that can be eaten whole plus the bones. Sardines have almost every nutrient that your body needs.

Carb content: zero.

Shellfish

Shellfish is one of the most nutritious foods that you can find on the menu, however, it is not part of the preferred list for many individuals. They are close to organ meats in terms of nutrient density and low in carbs.

Carb content: each 100 grams of shellfish contains 4 – 5 grams of carb.

Other Low Carb Fish and Seafood include: Haddock, Shrimp, Halibut, Herring, Catfish, Cod, Tuna, Lobster.

VEGETABLES

Most vegetables have low carb count especially greens and cruciferous vegetables with a high fiber content. While starchy root vegetables like sweet potatoes and potatoes have high carb counts.

Broccoli

Broccoli, a tasty cruciferous vegetable can be eaten either raw or cooked. It has high quantity of Vitamin C, K and fiber along with compounds that help to fight cancer.

Carb content: 7 grams in each 100 grams.

Tomatoes

Tomatoes though called berries or fruits can also be eaten as vegetables. Tomatoes are rich in potassium and vitamin C.

Carb Count: 4 grams in every 100 grams.

Onions

Apart from having a good taste, onions also add a great flavor to your recipes. Onions are rich in antioxidants, fiber as well as other anti-inflammatory compounds.

Carb Count: 9 grams in every 100 grams.

Brussels Sprouts

These are highly nutritious vegetables like the Kale and Broccoli. They are rich in Vitamins C and K and have other benefits.

Carb Count: 7 grams in every 100 grams.

Cauliflower

You can use Cauliflower to make different dishes. They are rich in Vitamins C, K and folate.

Carb Count: 5 grams in a cup and in every 100 grams.

Kale

People who are conscious of their health consume Kale a lot because of its various health benefits. The vegetable is rich in Vitamins C, k, fiber and carotene antioxidants.

Carb Count: 10 grams in every 100 grams.

Eggplants

This can be used to make different dishes and is rich in fiber.

Carb Count: 5 grams in every 100 grams.

Cucumber

This fruit is made up of mostly water with a little amount of vitamins K.

Carb Count: 4 grams in every 100 grams.

Bell Peppers

Rich in Vitamins C, fiber and carotene antioxidants. Has a satisfying but distinct flavor.

Carb Count: 6 grams in every 100 grams.

Asparagus

This is a spring vegetable rich in Vitamins C, K, fiber, folate and carotene antioxidants. When compared with other vegetables, this has a higher amount of protein.

Carb Count: 2 grams in every 100 grams.

Green Beans

Although these are legumes but they are treated as vegetables. Each calorie has rich amount of nutrients including protein, fiber, vitamins C, K, potassium and magnesium.

Carb Count: 7 grams in every 100 grams.

Mushrooms

Edible mushrooms are usually considered as vegetables. They are high in B vitamins as well as have a good amount of potassium.

Carb Count: 3 grams in every 100 grams.

Other low carb vegetables are Spinach, Celery, Cabbage, Swiss chard and Zucchini.

Apart from the starchy root vegetables, all other vegetables have low carb count. This is why there is no limit to your vegetable consumption.

FRUITS

Although fruits are healthy but may not be so beneficial to people on low carb diet as they have a higher amount of carbs when compared to vegetables. So, keep your fruit intake to 1 or 2 per day depending on the amount of carb you are aiming for.

These however does not apply to fatty fruits like olives and avocado. Also, low sugar berries like strawberries are another great choice.

Avocado

This is a special type of fruit that is high in fats rather than carbs. It is also rich in potassium and fiber and have a good amount of other nutrients.

Always keep in mind that about 78% of carbs found in avocado are actually fiber and so it has no digestible net carbs.

Carb Count: 8.5 grams in every 100 grams.

Olives

This is another delicious fruit with high fat content. It is rich in copper and iron and also some amount of vitamin E.

Carb Count: 6 grams in every 100 grams.

Strawberries

This is a fruit with the lowest carb count filled with nutrients, rich in manganese, vitamins C and other antioxidants.

Carb Count: 8 grams in every 100 grams.

Grapefruits

These are related to Oranges and are rich in carotene antioxidants and vitamin C.

Carb Count: 11 grams in every 100 grams.

Apricots

This is a very delicious fruit. While it has a little carb, it is rich in potassium and vitamins C.

Carb Count: 11 grams in every 100 grams.

Other low carb fruits are Kiwis, Lemons, Mulberries, Oranges and Raspberries

These are popular on the list as they are low in carbs but rich in fiber, fats, proteins and several micronutrients.

While you can eat nuts like snacks, seeds on the other hand can be added as crunch to salads or to any recipes.

Also, nut and seed flours like coconut flour, almond flour and flaxseed meal are sometimes used to make low carb breads and other baked foods.

Almonds

These are not only crunchy but also tasty. They are high in Vitamin E, fiber and magnesium.

Studies show that almonds help in weight loss and they also fill one up quickly.

Carb Count: 22 grams in every 100 grams.

Walnuts

This is another sweet nut that has different nutrients especially alpha-linolenic acid (ALA), omega-3 fatty acid.

Carb Count: 14 grams in every 100 grams.

Peanuts

Although these are legumes, however they are treated and eaten like nuts. They are rich in magnesium, fiber, vitamin E and other needed minerals and vitamins.

Carb Count: 16 grams in every 100 grams.

Chia Seeds

This tops the list of most popular healthy food in the world. They are rich in nutrients and added to different low carb recipes. They are also one of the richest sources of dietary fiber in the world.

It is important to note that 86% of carbs found in chia seeds are fiber which makes them digestible net carbs.

Carb Count: 44 grams in every 100 grams.

Other low carbs nuts and seeds are Cashews, Hazelnuts, Flaxseeds, Coconuts, Macadamia nuts, Pistachios, Sunflower seeds and Pumpkin seeds

DIARY

If you are not allergic to diary then full fat diary products makes up great low carb foods. Always read the labels and avoid foods with added sugar.

Cheese

Cheese is one of the tastiest meals in the low carb food list and it can be eaten raw on its own or added to any choice recipes. It combines well with meat like adding on top a bunless burger. It is rich in nutrients as a thick single slice have similar nutrient quantity as seen in a glass of milk.

Carb Count: 1.3 grams in every 100 grams.

Heavy Creams

This is low in carbs and protein but rich in diary fat. You can either add it to your coffee or use while making your recipes. One example of this is a bowl of berries and whipped cream.

Carbs count: 3 grams in every 100 grams.

Full fat Yogurt

These are extremely healthy and contain same nutrients found in whole milk.

It is also rich in probiotic bacteria.

Carbs count: 5 grams in every 100 grams.

Greek Yogurt

This is also referred to as strained yogurt and is thicker than the regular yogurt. It is rich with nutrients especially protein.

Carbs count: 4 grams in every 100 grams.

FATS AND OIL

While several healthy fats and oil make the list for low carb diet, you should avoid refined vegetable oils like the corn or soybean oil as they can be unhealthy if you consume excess of it.

Butter

Grass-fed butter has a higher count of certain nutrients.

Carbs count: zero

Extra Virgin Olive Oil

This is the healthiest of all the available fats in the world. It is rich in powerful antioxidants and anti-inflammatory compounds.

Carbs count: zero.

Coconut oil

This is another healthy fat that has medium-chain fatty acids that gives positive effects to our metabolism. The fatty acids help to boost fat burning, reduce appetite and as well lose belly fat.

Carbs count: zero.

Other low carb friendly fats include: Lard, Avocado oil and Tallow.

BEVERAGES

Most beverages that do not have sugar makes the low carb diet list. Note that fruit juices are rich in carbs and sugar and should be avoided.

Water

Irrespective of what your diet looks like, water is an important list for healthy living and weight loss.

Carbs count: zero.

Coffee

Coffee is not only healthy but also among the best sources of dietary antioxidants. Research has also proven that people that drive coffee live longer and has reduced risk of different serious diseases like Parkinson's disease, type 2 diabetes and Alzheimer. Best way to take your coffee is without adding anything but if you most, then make use of heavy cream or full-fat milk.

Carbs count: zero.

.

Tea

Studies over the years have shown that tea, especially green tea is packed with various health benefits, it may also boost burning of fat.

Carbs count: zero.

Club Soda/ Carbonated Water

This is simply water that has carbo dioxide added to it. Always read the label to confirm it has no added sugar.

Carbs count: zero.

Dark Chocolate

This may be surprising to you but quality dark chocolate makes the list of perfect low carb meals. It is important that these chocolates have at least 70 to 85% of cocoa to make sure that the sugar content is low. Part of the benefits of the dark chocolate include improved blood pressure and brain function.

From studies, we also gathered that people that consume dark chocolate have reduced risk of having any heart disease.

Note that 25% of carbs found in dark chocolate are fiber.

Carbs count: 46 grams in every 100 grams depending on the type. Always consult the label.

Herbs, Spices and Condiments

The list for delicious and beneficial spices, herbs and condiments are endless. The carb count in most of them are low and yet still packed with nutritional values while adding flavor to your dish. Some of these include pepper, ginger, salt, garlic, mustard, cinnamon and oregano.

CHAPTER 4

7 Days Low-Carb Menu Plan

This is a sample menu plan that would help you plan your meals for one week. It contains total carbs of less than 50 grams per day. Remember that you can increase your carb intake if you have no health challenge and you are physically active.

Sunday

- **Breakfast:** Omelet fried in coconut oil or butter that has various vegetables inside.

- **Lunch:** Grass-fed yogurt combined with blueberries and a few almonds.

- **Dinner:** Bunless cheeseburger, served with salsa sauce and vegetables.

Monday

- **Breakfast:** Bacon with eggs.

- **Lunch:** You can consume burgers and veggies remaining from the night before.

- **Dinner:** Salmon with vegetables and butter.

Tuesday

- **Breakfast:** Vegetables mixed inside eggs fried with coconut oil or butter.

- **Lunch:** Shrimp salad dipped with olive oil.

- **Dinner:** Grilled chicken and vegetables.

Wednesday

- **Breakfast:** Omelet with any vegetable combination, fried in coconut oil or butter.

- **Lunch:** A glass of smoothie that has berries, coconut milk, protein powder and almonds.

- **Dinner:** Veggies and steak.

Thursday

- **Breakfast:** Eggs with Bacon.

- **Lunch:** Chicken salad and some olive oil.

- **Dinner:** Pork chopped along with vegetables.

Friday

- **Breakfast:** Omelet with any vegetables' combination, fried in coconut oil or butter.

- **Lunch:** Grass-fed yogurt with coconut flakes, berries, and a few walnuts.

- **Dinner:** Veggies and Meatballs.

Saturday

- **Breakfast:** Fried eggs and Bacon.

- **Lunch:** A glass of smoothie with chocolate-flavored protein powder, coconut milk, berries and a dash of heavy cream.

- **Dinner:** Grilled chicken wings covered with some raw spinach by the side.

If you wish to work with less than 50 grams of carb daily, there is room for more veggies and then a fruit per day. Ensure to include as many low carb vegetables as possible.

CHAPTER 5

Conclusion

Low carb diets reduce the amounts of carbs that you can consume in meals such as the ones in processed foods, sugary products, bread and pasta. Low carb diet meals have high amount of fat, protein and lots of healthy vegetables.

From the meal plan in this book, you are able to know the basics of eating healthy low carb diets.

Consuming meals with low carb count would have a tremendous benefit on your health. Most foods under this list are nutritious, healthy and very sumptuous.

What's more, they cover several varieties of food including fish, meats, fruits, vegetables, diary products and so much more.

A healthy, low carb diet based on real or whole food would not only improve your general wellbeing but also help you shed unwanted weight.

Other Books by Nancy Peterson

Printed in Great Britain
by Amazon

24357545R00047